Smiles through the Mist
A Journey of No Return

Paul E Johnson

Copyright © 2017, Paul E. Johnson
All rights reserved.

No part of this book may be reproduced in any form or by any electronic or mechanical means, including information storage and retrieval systems, without permission in writing from the publisher, except by reviewers, who may quote brief passages in a review.

Published in Cary, North Carolina, United States of America

Library of Congress Control Number 2017915028

PREFACE	1
CHAPTER ONE	3
Reflections of Beginnings	
CHAPTER TWO	12
The Search	
CHAPTER THREE	21
Continued Support	
CHAPTER FOUR	27
The Journey Gets Tougher	
CHAPTER FIVE	42
Each Day an Adventure	
CHAPTER SIX	57
The 'A' Team is formed	
CHAPTER SEVEN	62
The Final Days	
CHAPTER EIGHT	72
The Celebration of a Life	

PREFACE

My personal struggle has changed my life way beyond what I had ever imagined. In telling my story of six years as a caregiver to my wife with Alzheimer's disease, you may find many instances of likeness to your own experiences, but each of us has to deal with it in his own way. This writing is my way.

However, we all experience the frustration from inadequate Alzheimer's research due to underfunding and the feeling of helplessness because of an unknown cure; finally, and most importantly, from the disappearance of one human being's total identity, that which makes them—them.

Acknowledgments

This book is dedicated to my beautiful wife Helene, the many Alzheimer's patients and their caregivers, and the families everywhere who have endured the pain and suffering of this dreaded disease. The Hospice team of professionals and my three private-duty CNAs (My "A" Team), the Duke and Rotary Club support groups, and my family and many friends both in North Carolina and elsewhere.

CHAPTER ONE

Reflections of Beginnings

I stared down at the empty, neatly made hospital bed. Placed at the head and centered was one light pink-colored faux rose. Attached to the rose stem was a paper containing a verse:

> When those we love go away,
> they never really leave us,
> they are with us now, wherever we are.
> Those whom we have cherished live on forever,
> for love wraps itself around the heart.

"Wow," I said to myself, "what just happened?" As though I had never seen this bed before, or the brightly lit front room I was standing in, facing the street in the house where we lived for the past seven years. The room Helene had been in since April 22nd when hospice took over her medical care.

Today was Saturday, May 20, 2017, about 10:30 a.m. The funeral home had just taken Helene from the house. The hospice nurse had pronounced her dead at 8:05 a.m., waited for them to arrive, then left. Helene's two daughters were in another part of the house, grieving. They were supposed to visit the following weekend for our anniversary on the twenty-eighth, but Helene's condition spoke to getting them here quicker, so I called them and they were able to get here from Connecticut in time to be by her side when she passed.

At a time like this your mind races about what's next—arrangements, contacts, and a sense of loneliness together with a lump in my throat like I had just swallowed an apple whole. I touched the bed and picked up the rose the funeral home had left. I thought this was a classy touch on their part. Helene was a classy lady and this would have been something she would have loved.

My thoughts started wandering to that period in the fall of 2011, a year after we moved to North Carolina from Connecticut for retirement, when I first started noticing something was not quite right with the way Helene was handling our bill payments which she did most of the time. She was always very astute with that kind of thing; after all, she had a degree in accounting and was a payroll supervisor for a major hospital in Connecticut. Her family was full of very smart people. Her oldest brother was a mechanical engineer and entrepreneur, the other was an MD, and the remaining nieces and nephews an assortment of lawyers, scientists, and the like.

Helene would make entries in the check register in the wrong columns for deposits and payments, pay the wrong vendors, pay wrong amounts, and her errors in arithmetic and bank statement reconciliations became a task for the two of us. I thought she was just having a bad day at first, but when I asked her about it, she would get annoyed with me and tell me she was fine.

In 2012 Helene brought new concerns which, when they first happened, seemed normal. We each had our own car and would at times do errands, meetings, and volunteering separately. She would leave the house to go on an errand to a place she had been before and although we'd been in NC for a year or so, she would come home after an extended amount of time and say she got lost or made a wrong turn somewhere.

At first, I thought nothing of it, as most everyone makes a wrong turn at times and gets lost. I'd kid her about it and she'd say, "Did you miss me"? or "We're retired and have plenty of time."

Then there's the trouble finding the right word or words trick which, of course, happens to all of us. We'd try to help each other out by filling in the blanks, but that in and of itself didn't seem to be a concern at the time.

The game of remembering names and dates was also not troubling at first either, as I myself, have forgotten the name of someone I just met, literally minutes after meeting them.

The next one of misplacing objects or "senior hide and seek" comes with the territory at this age, and again we all have our moments where we wish everything we owned had a tracking device on it.

Singularly, none of these things caused concern to me at first. Expectations of these things happening at age sixty-nine seemed to be fairly commonplace and initially masked the real culprit.

Helene did appear quieter, less vocal, than usual in groups of our friends. She was normally reserved but joined in conversations with a good sense of humor and contributed independently to any gathering, letting me be the wit.

We shared most everything together, from what and where to eat, vacation trips, and house furnishings, to movies we wanted to see. We'd usually go to a movie she'd want to see and then she'd join me to see one I wanted. She loved the romances, the mysteries, and musicals. I of course liked the guys' movies, the action, gunfights, car chases, and the alien SyFy. But something was changing; I wasn't sure what yet, but she seemed to be letting me make more of the decisions. She would say, "Whatever you want," or "I don't care; that's fine."

Helene started asking me what clothing she should wear. Usually, it was her decision and she would say, "How's this look?" or "Do you think I might need a sweater tonight?" Instead, she seemed at odds as to what to put on. She'd stand in the closet looking at her clothes and, after a few minutes, she'd turn to me and say, "What should I put on ?" and I would pick something out.

We usually did housecleaning together. We'd split up and clean the bathrooms, floors, and dusting, and threw in a few loads of clothes in the washing machine to boot. She usually left the ironing to me since I was fussy about dress shirts and creases in my pants. But she started asking me what to do. Her interest and "take charge attitude" seemed to be waning. She seemed to prefer me to assign a job to do rather than splitting up the tasks. I'd ask her if she felt all right or was she tired and wanted to postpone it for now, but she'd just say, "No, I'm fine. I'll help you."

Being accountants and in the world of finance, tax, and payroll, organizational skills were part of our lives. The traits followed us into our home as well, with neatness and "taking care of business," such as no dishes left in the sink, turning off the lights when leaving a room, putting things back where they belong, and paying bills before the due date. I know some would call us annul.

Helene started to leave the lights on in whatever room she left and left anything she put down in place or wherever she wanted without putting it back. I repeatedly asked her to put the lights out in the master bathroom after she was through, but the requests went unheeded, so I ended up installing a motion detection switch in the bathroom to automatically go off after a minute or so.

I found myself following her many times, putting things back, and turning lights off. In hindsight, however, I just should have left the lights on, but old habits die hard, and playing "senior hide and seek" was not getting to be as fun as it used to be, especially when she forgot where she had put her diamond engagement ring or when she left her pocketbook in a restaurant and by the time I asked her where it was and ran back from the parking lot to the booth where we were sitting, it was gone. I inquired of the staff but they said no one had seen it or turned it in.

In June 2012 we went on a land/cruise trip to Alaska, something we wanted to do for a while, and found a couple in our fifty-five-plus community who were planning to do the same trip that year. Bob and Mary were very nice people and a bit reserved like ourselves, but perhaps a bit more adventuresome on side tours. We flew into Fairbanks for our land excursion first, taking in the sights of Mt McKinley, Denali Park, and Eskimo Villages. We panned for gold and actually captured a few flakes of the stuff—it was fun. We ate meals together and had a great time.

The side tours we picked, however, split us up due to the more adventuresome side of Bob and Mary (at least Bob). All four of us chose white water rafting which involved a choice of a few levels of rapids. Helene and I kept with the level 1 which was calmer rapids and less "splash." That was okay with us since the water was 34 degrees Fahrenheit in June and even though we had protective clothing the tour guides gave us; we trod on the side of caution.

Our tour partners chose level 4, which may have been one level below total self-destruction, but they came out of it fine and we got pictures to prove it. The other side tour we got split up on was the choice between visiting a musher's camp to see the sled dogs or ATV-riding over rough terrain. Yeah, that's right, you guessed it—we chose the musher's camp and Bob and Mary chose the ATV tour.

This time we chose correctly as the ATV tipped over on Mary (they each rode their own) and it took some time to get over the bruises.

The second half of the trip coming back was the cruise from Whittier, Alaska, to Vancouver, Canada. We upgraded to a veranda suite on the ship and it proved to be worthwhile to see the icebergs calving and crashing into the inlet.

We had chosen meal plans prior to sailing. We chose the open seating plan, meaning we sat with whomever was seated with us that night. Unknown to us, Bob and Mary had chosen the traditional plan which meant they would sit with the same people at their table every night. Since we were cruising together, that arrangement was not going to work not only because of not eating together but also missing a chance to meet other people on the cruise.

Bob and Mary decided to join our open seating plan and got permission, which worked out for the reason mentioned, but would add more clues to Helene's impending condition which had yet to be diagnosed. During the trip besides eating together, we often sat in many parts of the ship for dancing, shows, or simply to have a drink and listen to the piano player. At these times, I had occasion to leave the three of them and go to the restroom or perhaps check on a reservation at one of the restaurants on the ship.

Mary would tell me later that Helene would start looking around for me, possibly a bit pensive; when I wasn't back momentarily, she'd seemed to get quiet and avoid conversation when I was gone.

I'd ask her later if she was okay and she'd reply, "Fine," or say, "You were gone a long time." I was a bit surprised by her answer but nonetheless paid more attention to my absences for the remainder of the trip.

In August we drove to Connecticut and Massachusetts for a visit with family and friends. Helene's two daughters Laura and Jennifer mentioned noticing the loss of finding the words and the confusion of times, places, or people. Recently more of our friends had noticed and mentioned the same thing. It became clear to me that this was becoming more than just a passing attribute of getting older: it needed the attention of our family doctor.

CHAPTER TWO
The Search

September 2012 Helene and I sat down for "that discussion." We both knew things weren't right and we had to find the answer for both of us. Feelings ran high and we did a lot of hugging and she got upset. I knew she was afraid and deep down I was too, but I did not show too much emotion until I was sure what was happening.

We saw our GP, Dr. R, on September 14th. Helene was quite upset in his office, but not being a specialist, all he could do was to refer us to a local neurologist in town. On Sept 27th we visited the neurologist, Dr. J. He asked Helene the standard questions, i.e. today's date, month, year, and who the president was.

Helene hesitated at times but answered most of the doctor's questions correctly. I could tell she was a bit annoyed at his questioning and possibly wasn't crazy about him personally, but we got through it. At the end of the visit, Dr. J recommended getting an MRI at the local hospital. He also prescribed an over-the-counter pill called

BACOMIND, taken daily for cognitive and sleep support, and Axona, a powder to be mixed with milk to support metabolic processes associated with mild to moderate impairment.

On October 1, 2012, Helene received an MRI from the local hospital. We asked for and received a disk with her brain images on it. We took this to our appointment on October 4th, revisiting Dr. J., who did not elaborate on any unusual findings except a growth called an acoustic neuroma (cauliflower-shaped about, 2 ½ centimeters) in Helene's left ear canal. He suggested a consult with a neurosurgical clinic about the ear growth and a follow-up visit in January 2013.

On October 9th we visited the neurosurgeon, Dr. M, relating to the ear growth. He pointed to three possible paths for this since it may affect Helen's hearing: wait to see if it grows larger, if not leave it alone; a laser treatment to stop or inhibit growth; or lastly, operate, which has serious risks attached, namely permanent deafness. Dr. M also set up an audiology test nearby.

November came and Helene's appetite had decreased. Often after making dinner for us, she would eat little of it. I kept having to remind her to take her prescribed medications which she did not like at all. Her cooking was also starting to be a challenge in that under- or overcooking was frequent. Putting clothes away also was a challenge by mixing hers with mine.

I called Dr. M's office on November 13th to follow up on his receiving the audiology report and his thoughts on next steps. His office had no word yet and told me to call back in a week. I also called Dr. J's office about Helene's tolerance to the prescriptions she was taking. I also asked whether there was something else she could try.

Dr. J's office returned my call the next day, advising me to restart the meds all over only in smaller doses to build up tolerance, but nothing about an alternative medication. They set up an appointment for January 10, 2013, to follow up.

I called Dr. M's office again on November 19th. The assistant said she would get back to me the next day. Dr. M's office called as promised and suggested a second opinion with Dr. F, another neurosurgeon at a clinic nearby.

On Nov 26th Dr. F's office called and set up an appointment for Helene for January 14, 2013, and to bring our copy of the MRI disc to review.

January 10, 2013, came and Dr. J's appointment consisted of recommending a full workup at the Duke

Memory Clinic in Durham. His office made an appointment for Wednesday, April 10th. He also prescribed Aricept and Namenda, both cognitive support medications for memory.

On January 14th we visited Dr. F's office. We were very impressed by his consultation and what appeared to be many plaques and honors in different languages on his walls. He showed us a display of the head without the brain and the area of where the acoustic neuroma was and what nerves it was touching. He also explained he could only remove 90 percent of the tumor as anything more could cause injury to the facial nerves and permanent loss of hearing on the left side. The operation would proceed in March 2013 due to his being out of the country.

On January 17th, my first real scare and portent of the future came to us as a couple. All the things I had held deep within me came to the surface and I knew we were about to have our lives changed forever. I went bowling between 12:00 and 3:30 p.m. that day. Since we were expecting a storm that day (rain then snow), I told Helene to stay home since she had nothing planned except maybe a library volunteer job less than a mile from our house. I was concerned that a trip in the car alone any further than the library may get her confused and lost.

It turned out I was right. I got home about 3:30 p.m. and discovered Helene's car was gone. I went into the house through the garage and found the front door wide open, no note, and her cell phone still on the dresser. I called around to some of the neighbors and the library with no luck. The weather was getting nasty outside and getting darker. I was beside myself on next steps, thinking she may turn up any moment or should I call the police.

I was gazing out the window toward the street contemplating when a police car pulled up in front of the house. It was about 4:50 p.m. I looked in the backseat of the cruiser from the window and saw Helene sitting there. I immediately rushed outside toward the police cruiser as the policeman was helping Helene out of the back. I saw the tears streaming down her face. She looked afraid. The policeman got her to the sidewalk and I hugged her. "I went for a ride," she said, "and got lost on NC55. I am sorry."

She was only one and a half miles from the house but had the sense to pull into a gas station where a policeman was parked. She told him she was lost and needed directions and he decided the best thing to do was bring her home. I told her to go into the house and I would ask the officer for a ride back to the gas station to get her car and bring it back home. The policeman agreed and I went with him and retrieved the car. After that incident, I knew our path together was not going to be easy.

On January 30th we returned to Dr. M's office. We were told the operation was going forward on February 22 (originally told March) at a hospital in Raleigh. There would be a pre-op visit on February 15th. We went to the pre-op visit with no problems.

On February 22nd the operation was performed. It took seven hours and about 90–95 percent of the tumor was removed. I was fortunate to have good friends and neighbors in our community. A friend from my street offered to sit with me in the waiting room for the first four hours. I was a nervous wreck. Both Dr. M and Dr. F did the operation together. They had to enter the skull from in back of her left ear to get to the tumor. When the operation was finally over, Dr. M appeared dressed in the full operating garb from head to toe, but the best part was the very large grin on his face I will never forget it. I knew he was pleased and I had a sigh of relief inside. No nerve damage was done and the operation was a complete success.

On March 10th the stitches were removed and the healing process and hair growth back continued. On March 14th we visited Dr. M again. He was extremely pleased with the results and progress Helene had made. He made a final appointment for May 8th and would make an appointment at the hospital for a final MRI before the office visit. Unfortunately, the removal of the tumor had no effect on the memory issues Helene was having.

On April 10th we visited the Duke Memory Clinic in Durham. We met Dr. S. We gave him Helene's medical history, including her immediate family information. The doctor asked her the standard questions (day, month, year, etc.) as well as three words to remember for later and asked her to spell the word "world" backwards.

Helene remembered two of the three words, but could not spell the word "world" backwards. Dr. S told us she definitely had a memory issue and wanted to run more tests. Five vials of blood were drawn for testing: apolipoprotein (APOE) genotyping, CBC with auto differential, comprehensive metabolic panel, folate RPR, thyroid profile, and vitamin B12. The results would be discussed at the next appointment on May 15th.

On May 8th we went to the hospital for the follow-up MRI as requested by Dr. M. We received a copy of the disk of the views and proceeded to Dr. M's office for the appointment. He was very pleased with the report from the hospital on the MRI and released Helene as "cured." He then wanted her back after a year to see if any growth of the remaining tumor had occurred. If so, Helene would get a dose of radiation to stop the growth and then he gave us a prescription for an audiology exam follow-up.

On May 13th we went back to the audiology appointment to test Helene again after the operation to see if the hearing had changed. The results from the audiologist confirmed a severe loss of hearing on the left side and that hearing aides were strongly recommended. We then ordered two digital hearing aids. An appointment for May 21st was made for a fitting of the hearing aids.

On May 15th we returned to Duke and Dr. S for results of the blood tests. Despite all other tests showing Helene was healthy, such as kidney, liver, blood pressure, and even the gene to determine if she passed on anything to her kids, she was diagnosed with Alzheimer's disease.

After the May 15th appointment, Helene became depressed over the fact she was not able to drive her car. She became more forgetful of her address, phone number, her kids' birthdays, and the thoughts of possibly entering a nursing home or dying in the next few years. My support did little to allay these fears so, after contacting Dr. S at

Duke, we decided to visit a psychiatrist in Raleigh he recommended that might be able to help.

From May 13th through July, Helene tried the new hearing aids but to no avail. She found them annoying and uncomfortable and insisted she didn't need them except for restaurants because of the ambient noise and did not wear them. So, I took them back and got most of my money back.

On August 28th we saw a clinical nurse named Mary at the psychiatrist's office. She listened to Helene for about an hour. Helene said she wanted to be prescribed a medication for her depression. Since Mary was not qualified to prescribe, I made my next appointment with one of the psychiatrists for September 18th. That way if he thought she needed a prescription, he could authorize it.

CHAPTER THREE
Continued Support

On Sept 8–16, 2013, we went upstate to visit family and friends in Connecticut and Massachusetts. Helene did fine, but traveling by car was getting more difficult, and stopping on the way in public places was very hard. When we got there, everyone noticed the changes in Helene, especially since they hadn't seen her for a while.

On Sept. 18, 2013, we visited Dr. Z, the psychiatrist in Raleigh, for the first time. I sat in on the meeting on the couch with Helene. Dr. Z was a quiet man, talking to Helene and listening to her between her bouts of sadness and being upset. She frequently needed tissues and told him of her feeling bad about herself and her condition. I also spoke to him and consoled her, holding her hand and trying to fill in any needed information to help him decide on the appropriate medication or solutions. At the end of our meeting, he prescribed Sertraline (Zoloft) 25 mg daily to start with, with adjustments as needed, and set a new appointment for Oct 18th, between Oct 2–Nov 6, 2013 (5 weeks) from 2:00–5:00 p.m. Helene and I joined an Alzheimer's support group in Durham, put on by the Duke Memory Clinic. Since we were both able to attend together and meet other caregivers and patients, Helene enjoyed being among those with the same issues. We'd get guest speakers, share our own experiences, and get help from others with references. Social workers led the activities. We'd meet once a month at a local restaurant in a private room, have lunch, and go around the room telling everyone what was happening in our lives and getting advice from each other on aspects of concern. We became an extended family, revealing very personal things we wouldn't share with the outside world. This process of meetings, lunches, special events (museum exhibits), seminars, and "memory cafes" continued with either both of us or later just myself through 2017.

Oct 18, 2013, we visited Dr. Z. The meeting was much the same as the first one, with sadness, crying, and hand-holding. No significant changes were noted, but the sadness issue did not seem to be getting any better and he told me to call if I thought an increase from 25 mg of Sertraline to 50 mg might be in order.

As the month went on the sadness issue seemed to elevate, so I called and he increased the dosage to 50 mg daily.

On March 12, 2014, we visited Dr. S at Duke for a follow-up visit. The doctor seemed pleased there were no significant changes to Helene's condition and told us he was going to leave the appointments "open," but to call him if anything had changed. I thought, Well, since there is no cure for this disease, he feels "no news is good news." I guess it is the protocol here. We later found out from internal sources at Duke that the doctor was retiring in May of that year. That made me a bit angry as he did not even mention that fact to us and we ultimately were left without being referred to someone else. I guess he figured that Dr. J would handle it.

May 28th was our wedding anniversary. We typically went somewhere special each year, usually in the spring/summertime frame and somewhere in Europe or elsewhere for at least two weeks, besides our normal trips to see family and friends and a few days at points of interest in the US. Helene loved to travel and I loved to go with her. We always had fun meeting people and discovering "how the other half lived" as they used to say. We took many pictures and put them in albums to show friends or look at ourselves later. I didn't realize it then, but it would become important later on, using them to look at as Helene's disease progressed and a search for memories became much more important.

So on May 5–15, 2014, we took our trip to celebrate our twenty-fifth wedding anniversary. We chose a cruise to the Mediterranean (Turkey, Greece, Cypress, and Israel, with a visit to Bethlehem and Jerusalem). We hadn't been there yet and although we were rather "relaxed" with our faith (Helene was Jewish and I was Christian (Episcopal), that part of the world was steeped in history about religion and faith. I felt, too, that because of what Helene and I were going through, this could possibly bring us more understanding spiritually. That verdict is still out.

Despite a few glitches on the trip itself—a seven-hour delay at the Raleigh airport due to plane mechanical repair and a ship propeller malfunction, due possibly to a fishing net tangle on it, which we never really found out—Helene did pretty well. I was, however, on high alert in public places such as ladies' restrooms and on tours over rough terrain such as cobblestone streets and burial sites, due to Helene's propensity for falling or bumping into things. It turns out this would be the last trip Helene and I would ever take outside of North Carolina.

Chapter Three

On May 21, 2014, we revisited Dr. J's office and met with Kelly, FNP, instead of the doctor. Helene and I liked her. She made Helene seem more relaxed and she told us she'd stay in touch with Dr. M for a possible MRI follow-up. The follow-up appointment for the MRI was made for Sept 26th in the hospital annex in the town of Apex next to ours, and Dr. M's visit would be on Oct 9th.

Helene has been doing okay day to day. Her hearing is still in need of assistance, but she only complains in crowds or restaurants. Her dependency on me grows more each day, as does her sensitivity to my emotions. If I raise my voice at times to show aggravation about our circumstances, she cries. I then, of course, felt bad and tried to explain to her that it was the disease that I was mad at, not her. But this month (May), I did hire a companion (Carol) recommended by our close friend Mary in the community to stay with Helene while I went bowling once each week, or volunteered with my civic group assisting in police activities for our town. I could not leave Helene alone anymore and it gave me an outlet.

Helene's daughters came to visit us on Oct 4–5, 2014 for the weekend. Helene was pleased to see them, although her conversational acumen was continuing to decline so the kids had to ask questions or prompt her to get a response.

On October 9, 2014, we revisited Dr. M's office for a follow-up view of Helene's MRI taken on Sept 26th. The findings were normal, with a slight spot at the operation sight. A follow-up in 2015 was ordered. If the findings were also good, Helene's case would be closed.

On October 15, 2014, we visited Dr. J's office for review of the Alzheimer's meds; the continuation of Aricept and Namenda would remain.

CHAPTER FOUR

The Journey Gets Tougher

The year 2015 saw a continued decline in Helene's health and state of mind. Her emotions were more highly sensitized. She became more physical with her hands and feet (hitting, kicking, and throwing) and more frustrated with her abilities to do things on her own. She was more confused, saying phrases like "I can't do this" over and over again, and became unable to tell time or write her own name. Since she could not be left alone, my ability to do the normal day-to-day errands, shopping, even bill-paying, was becoming unmanageable because Helene's attention needs were ever present and I couldn't be alone in the room without her shadowing me everywhere. She showed no interest in reading, TV, or even walking around the block.

Our periodic semi-annual exams (February and August) with Dr. J our neurologist, were uneventful and short. He would ask the same questions (time, day, date, etc.) and then make an appointment with us for six months. We didn't get to see Kelly, his FNP, again due to pregnancy. I knew no cure equals, wait for the next shoe to drop before adjusting meds, but a lack of synergy between Helene and the doctor's personality had something to do with his short appointments.

Our psychiatrist Dr. Z was caring and compassionate and initially his prescriptions of Sertraline did help Helene, but her ongoing mental condition would prove a challenge to the various meds that would be prescribed by him going forward.

Our Duke Support Team affiliation was very worthwhile in that the gatherings and activities were initially welcomed by Helene. Duke's affiliation with the Nasher Museum afforded a chance to not only interact with others in our group but contribute personal opinions and feelings about the exhibitions shown us by their selected docents and get a chance at times to create our own artwork with materials supplied by the museum. We also had various forms of entertainment, either musical or artistic, to round out our experiences. Helene, until 2017, thoroughly enjoyed the experiences, but with the decline in health, both mentally and physically, could not attend. I, however, did attend even after her death as a part of my healing process.

There were other venues we attended with friends in the same situation, usually providing a meal and entertainment. Until the last year, Helene enjoyed them all.

I took Helene wherever I could: dinners with friends, entertainment venues, movies, etc., keeping her socialized and connected with the world as much as possible. Some she enjoyed, some not so much, becoming more disconnected with conversations with those she was with and coping with everyday decisions. I was becoming more exhausted in my efforts to please. Sleep at night was restless and little.

On September 1, 2015, I enrolled Helene in a daycare in Raleigh two days a week. It was another way I could manage my time and at the same time keep Helene active and safe in an environment with others. She seemed to enjoy it, making friends and having activities such as crafts, music, and lunch. Initially, I arranged to take her and pick her up. The staff was great and became good friends, always kidding Helene and me about being a great couple and complimenting Helene on how nice she looked each day with coordinating outfits, makeup, and hairstyles. The staff were informative and supportive, and the director was friendly and eager to please. On the way home we would talk about her day with friends and activities there and if she made something she would share all this with me. However, changes would be apparent as time passed and adjustments to cope with these changes were imminent.

On December 1st, I took Helene to a colon and rectal surgeon referred to me by our GP Dr. R, because I noticed what appeared to be a distention on the left side of Helene's stomach. He said it was a hernia due to a colon surgery in 2004, and common with this kind of surgery. He said based on her condition, unless she had discomfort in the area, to leave it alone.

I also called Dr. Z in December about Helene's increased anxiety by lashing out. He increased the Sertraline dosage from 50 to 75 mg daily. This was only the beginning of a list of a combination of drugs to cope with Helen's ever-changing mental dilemma.

I received a letter from Dr. J, the neurologist, in December, stating he was not going to take any more Medicare patients, not even the ones like Helene who were current patients. He said if we wanted to continue with his services, we would have to pay full fare. We in turn called Duke since the original diagnoses came from one of their doctors and asked if we could join their services. They called us back and said effective March 14, 2016, they would

Chapter Four

take us as Medicare patients and assign us to a fine neurologist from their staff, Dr. B.

The year 2016 brought more decline in Helene's health and a more aggressive strategy of medications, increased outside care, and my commitment to keep her with me at home. Although there seemed to be an increasing number of care facilities in the surrounding area from assisted living to continuing care, which included specific memory care units, the costs associated with these facilities are extremely expensive. The caliber of care in these facilities is also a concern for me.

Helene and I have visited a few of these facilities. Although their accommodations and services vary from place to place, their marketing is based more on independent living with attention to chef-prepared meals, luxury surroundings, and active adult activities. Each additional service provided to each resident is an additional cost which can mean additional hundreds to thousands of dollars per month, to say nothing about what happens to someone in these facilities who can no longer maintain an "active lifestyle"—they are asked to leave.

The staffing, although maybe adequate for active individual residents, falls short when dealing with dementia patients. Ratios of one staff member for every five, six, or seven dementia patients cannot nearly address the attention required. My personal experience taking care of my wife on a day-to-day basis for the last six years is evidence enough for anyone who has done it. Educational levels, experience, and dedication in this business are key and in order to make a profit these facilities can't or won't do it.

At the risk of sounding too political, this country has to address health care ASAP. The baby boomers retiring now will face this dilemma in a very short period of time (if they haven't already). Since the savings, retirement income, and costs of living are problematic for most retired individuals now, being able to afford the kind of facilities currently being erected will not help these people. We will be faced with either bringing these patients home for care or a deterioration of the places needed to house these people.

In January 2016, I enlisted an accredited Home Healthcare Agency from a listing put out by the Department of Health and Human Services in North Carolina. I was interviewed at home so they could evaluate Helene, me, and my home. They then told me they would send out possibly four different individuals at different times I needed care. This was done to acquaint each with Helene and me, for a "proper" fit.

Chapter Four

I assumed being a large agency they could provide me with a person at first, a few times a month, then, as need required, I would increase the days/hours to possibly full-time. Well, I was wrong. After a request for three to four visits of approximately four hours each (Jan–Mar), I requested someone for three hours in April for the evening of my police volunteer group meeting a week in advance.

A few days later, they called and said they couldn't find anyone to do it. It appears there weren't enough hours for anyone to make it "worthwhile" to come. I was surprised—maybe I shouldn't have been—but their potential for my increased business to full-time for who knows how long was good due to Helene's disease.

I dropped the agency and found a couple of very good private-duty people through a good friend of mine in my community to fill the gap for my meetings and bowling and a much-needed body massage once a month. I still had the daycare for Helene for only two days a week at that time.

Although we didn't travel outside NC anymore, Helene got daily calls from Laura and Jennifer and weekly Skype calls on Fridays. This kept the kids not only talking to their mother but seeing her on Skype made a visual impression of her appearance. We also talked about them flying down from Connecticut and visiting on weekends more.

On May 2, 2016, I increased the daycare from two days a week to three (Mon, Wed, Fri) and added a transportation feature of the daycare services. I had them pick her up in the morning (8:00 a.m.) for an additional charge and I would still pick her up in the late afternoon (4:00 p.m.), but still beating the going-home rush hour after 5:00 p.m. I hated that daily traffic when I was working. Helene adapted pretty well.

On May 24–27, 2016, we went to the Outer Banks of NC with another couple, Bob and Jayne. Jayne also had Alzheimer's, and we met through the Duke Support Group and its many gatherings. We also attended other Memory Cafes in the area. Bob was a volunteer in my police group. He had been to the OBX years before. Helene and I talked of going there and since Jayne was also in the same daycare as Helene and they became friends there, it seemed like a good fit, especially under the circumstances. We drove out to Kill Devil Hills, almost to the top of the island, the trip taking about more than four hours to drive. I volunteered to drive and Bob was my copilot. Even though he hadn't been out there for years, he was a great help and the ladies sat in the back and enjoyed the view talking to each other in low tones. I couldn't hear much, but they seemed to be having a good time. We got to the motel on the beach we had reservations for, with adjoining rooms for convenience, and started our tour.

We visited Currituck Beach Lighthouse, the adjacent Roanoke Island's Festival Park showing a settlers' village and sailing ship (Elizabeth II); Jeanette's Pier on the beach, stopping at O'Neal's Sea Harvest Restaurant for lunch; then on to Kitty Hawk to see the Wright Brothers National Memorial and Museum.

Next, we visited Jockey's Ridge State Park, then dinner at the Jolly Roger; Bodie Island Lighthouse; Pea Island National Wildlife Refuge, and stopped at Wacky Jack's Burger Shack for lunch. We continued to the Chicamacomico Complex, a US Life Saving Station and Museum which is also a National Heritage site. Finally, we arrived at Rodanthe, a small town with a famous house in the 2008 movie, Nights in Rodanthe, with Richard Gere, Diane Lane, and Viola Davis. We got a lot of great pictures and memories of our last trip in North Carolina.

At this date, June 13, 2016, Helene appears to have lost any remnants of independence. She shadows me everywhere I go in the house and has, at times, problems finding the bathroom. She appears to be paranoid about me leaving her and tells me I don't love her. She is confused as to whether we're married and thinks I have another home somewhere. She asks me whether I am staying for the night. She tells me I want to get rid of her and "put her somewhere."

Helene is starting to ask me, "Does Paul know about this?" in conversations with me and appears to be surprised at times when I say, "I am Paul." She is more often sad and cries more. Her phrases most often spoken now are, "I don't know what to do," "Now what do I do?" and "I am trying." She uses "They said" when telling me something and when I ask, "Who is they?" she tells me she doesn't know.

Helene is very unsteady on her feet and prone to falling if I am not there to stabilize her. I make all the decisions for her on everything including what to eat and drink at restaurants. She still remembers her two brothers, mother and father and daughters in pictures, and when the kids Skype each week. The oldest memories are the longest-lasting.

July 1, 2016, I increased the daycare from three days a week to five. The transportation is still being done in the mornings but I am getting us up at 5:30 a.m. now in order to get her ready for her 8:00 a.m. pickup. I know 2 ½ hours to get ready seems like more time than I need, but getting her into the shower, depending on the day, is not always easy. Our shower can only hold one of us, so I stand outside with the door just slightly open so she hears me over the water noise.

She at times fights me to get in (due to Helene's incontinence, showering each day is a must). Then instructions begin of getting the soap, what to wash, shampoo or not, getting rinsed off, then getting her out of the shower requires some delicate positioning (I added another grab handle) and finally, toweling dry. I then must dress her (I'd pick out her outfits the night before), blow dry and style her hair and put her makeup on. I take her to the living room, turn on the TV for the news and *Good Morning America* to keep her occupied while I shower, get dressed, and make us some breakfast (I set the table for that the night before also).

Not sleeping well at night doesn't help either. Helene has had sinus, allergies, and sleep problems for years. I exhausted the sleep studies, C-PAP machines, and custom-made oral dental devices to open her airways, none of which she could tolerate.

She snores like a trooper but seems to be sound asleep in spite of it. She also gets up once or twice a night for the bathroom which I must assist her with. I, on the other hand, have tried earplugs, sleeping in another room, and going to bed earlier (the last two I can't do any more for fear she needs me). All these so I can do things during the day.

Her increased depression and anger issues to everyone around her prompted me to call Dr. Z and schedule an office visit for July 29th. Up to now her prescription of Zoloft seemed to be keeping things under control, but the doctor agreed an addition of a small dosage of an antipsychotic (Buspirone) may help and he sent in a prescription. Helene was starting to hit not only me but also others around her. She would bang her head into walls at home and daycare. Many times, she would question whether anyone was coming to get her at daycare and wouldn't believe them when they told her I was coming.

She felt insecure at daycare at times and told them no one cared for her. The staff would try and assure her that she was loved and would make her paper hearts with a red yarn necklace to put around her neck to comfort her with the words "You are loved" or "You are cared for" written on the heart. I must have had more than a dozen of those. I also printed a picture of myself with the words, "I will pick you up at 4:00 p.m. today, Love Paul" with X's and O's underneath the picture in a small note fashion. Then I gave them to the staff to give to her on those unassured days to remind her of my arrival that day.

One of the daycare staff members who had spent probably the most time with Helene related her observations to me: "When Helene first arrived at our facility, she was very shy and quiet. Fortunately, another woman started at daycare around the same time Helene did. The two women bonded almost immediately—it was rare to see one without the other. They went to activities together, ate together, and were always almost side by side.

"Although neither one of them could actually play bingo, they went faithfully every day and seemed to enjoy themselves as long as they were together. Several months down the road, the other woman left the daycare. I believe Helene found her absence very upsetting. While she did have a few new relationships with other participants, none were the same close relationship she had with the woman who left. Helene remained much within herself. Her primary concern was Paul and when he was picking her up to go home.

"She did participate in some activities (exercise and singing)‹ although getting her to go to bingo was almost impossible. Gradually, Helene's behavior changed and she became angry very easily. On many of these occasions, I would sit with Helene and try to engage her in some activities. On a good day, she would read through magazines with me and we would pick out pictures of food or flowers and I tried to find out what foods she enjoyed or what flowers she liked.

"We used the magnetic spelling board to spell out everything from people's names to states and holidays. Helene knew her letters and if I asked her to find a "k" or a "b," she did so very quickly. She was very pleased when she was able to find the letters and smiled broadly. Generally, this activity would keep Helene occupied for an hour or two. One-on-one worked well with Helene—she was able to remain focused and relatively calm.

"Helene liked quiet and tranquility. Loud noises upset her, so I tried to keep her in a quiet setting which was not always easy. Sometimes after lunch, I would rub hand cream on her hands and massage them a bit. She enjoyed this activity and once in a while she would actually close her eyes and rest. This was a good time of the day for Helene.

She was still very concerned that Paul wouldn't come to pick her up, but constant reassurance put her at ease for a time. Dealing with Helene did grow harder as time moved on. Other staff members spent time with her, as sometimes my magic didn't work. The time spans of activity were much shorter, but kudos to my coworkers who tried to come up with things to do to keep Helene occupied. Working with Helene was a group effort: sometimes it worked, sometimes it didn't, as is true of so many folks here at daycare. I can honestly say we all gave it our best shot."

October 6, 2016, due to her unsteadiness, I decided to invest in a walker. I wanted Helene to walk more around the neighborhood on sidewalks to help strengthen her legs and maybe have better circulation. I believed in the slogan, "Use 'em or lose 'em." I checked out the different ones and decided on a walker/transporter. This, I thought, would give the stability of a walker with the added feature of (with a few adjustments) a transporter for short distances, to push her home if she got too tired. It had hand brakes, a seat, and a storage compartment under the seat. Medicare paid some (the cost of the cheapest walker). Needless to say, after only a few weeks and walks with me or my team it stopped.

As with all drugs of this nature, finding the right one for each patient is sometimes very difficult and by October 11th we were on to a new one called Seroquel. After altering dosages of this drug, we were no further ahead and by November 7th we again tried a different one called Risperidone. This drug seemed to have a better result, at least for the remainder of 2016.

CHAPTER FIVE
Each Day an Adventure

Each day now seems to be an adventure as to what will happen with Helene's temperament—smiling and congenial or combative and hateful. Whether she will say something new or lose more ability to do the simple things in life we all take for granted. The fear lives with me 24/7.

November 2016 brought the holidays upon us with Thanksgiving. Since we didn't have any family in NC, we were graciously invited to Ruby and Bill's house to have Thanksgiving dinner with their family. Ruby and Bill were part of our Duke Family Support Team. Ruby was Bill's caregiver and they made it nice to be there for the day.

The holidays were always hectic even at the daycare facility. Arts and crafts seemed to be the theme usually but during the holidays more so. Helene's days there were filled with things to do, like dancing, puzzles, games (card and active), finding new friends to talk to, or helping the staff with projects. Lunch was served at noon. She got her fingernails polished sometimes or for a fee. She could even get her hair cut and colored from a hairdresser who came in a couple of times a month. We had visited a few other daycare facilities in our town but this one in Raleigh had the best fit for me.

It had been just over a year now since Helene was at the daycare in Raleigh. She had adjusted well and seemed to enjoy her days for the most part. It took me about a 25–30-minute commute from my home to get her at 4:00 p.m. I would enter the reception area and greet whoever was sitting at the desk. Either a receptionist or one of the staff was usually there, but there was a monitor signaling a visitor if no one was there, so there was little wait time. The director's office was just off the reception area and I would often talk to her about Helene's day there. She later was the one who picked up Helene in the morning, due to her home being in close proximity to ours.

One of the staff would get Helene and bring her to the reception area. When they opened the door (locked for the safety of the clients), the first thing Helene saw was me standing there. Her eyes would usually light up as though she was far away and then discovered someone she knew and a smile would cover her face—like "smiles through the mist." I would say, "I am here to pick up my date." She would sometimes say, "I didn't expect you this soon" or turn to a staff member and say, "Have you met my husband?" or "I am glad you're here." To see the happiness on her lovely face made my day. The staff called us "the lovebirds" and would ask me what was planned for supper that night. I'd say, "Something romantic."

Depending on the weather or season, I would help her on with her coat or sweater (she usually wore a sweater—she was cold most of the time) and lead her to the car parked just outside. I'd help her in the car, buckled her up, and then bent down and gave her a kiss on the lips. She would smile and I'd close the car door.

We drove home talking about our day. I'd tell her about my errands or bowling and she'd tell me about the friends she sat with, never remembering their names, or tell me about someone she didn't like very much and tell me she would stay away from them. Helene was always wanting to help with what was going on. I understood that since she was a volunteer for many years. She was particularly pleased when a staff member would ask her to help them.

Although they served lunch each day around noon (the food was brought in), when I'd ask her what she had for lunch, she would always say, "I didn't eat lunch." The daycare did have a monthly calendar of events each day which they passed out so I could refer to it, but her memory could not relate. They displayed the lunch menu on the desk of the receptionist so I knew.

December 2016 brought more holidays, Christmas and Hanukkah. Although as I said we were "relaxed" on religion, we still observed both, with tree decorating and candle-lighting, with prayers and sending out holiday cards. In past years I'd put the tree up and put the lights on. The tree did have hardwired fiber optic lights on it as well. The tree was only 4 feet tall and artificial. We'd trim the tree together, usually a week or so before Christmas day, calling it, "our memory tree" as we had ornaments from places we'd been on vacations in foreign lands as well as the US. Helene loved to do it, unwrapping each ornament gently and trying to remember what country or state we got it from before placing it strategically on the tree.

For Hanukkah, we would light the Menorah each night for eight nights and Helene would say the Hebrew prayers while doing so. I tried pronouncing the words myself but I always went to the English translation. This year I said the prayers for her (in English). She looked at me, her face glowing in the candlelight, and said, "I love you."

In December I hired two caregivers to come and help me for the weekends for about six hours each day. They were very caring and gave me a chance to see a movie or go out with friends. This year I set the tree up, did labels for the holiday cards, and my two additional caregivers I hired for Saturdays and Sundays helped Helene with the cards and the tree trimming. She enjoyed it while I took some downtime.

January 2017, another year has arrived. I dread what this year will bring. My caregivers are here each weekend. Helene's daycare becomes my bastion for some rest and the normalcy of life. Yet I miss her in this house. I can't wait to see her at night. Sometimes I leave early to pick her up at daycare. Then I sit in the parking lot and wait until 3:50 p.m. before I walk in. As soon as I walk in and the staff sees me, someone goes to get her.

I engage in conversation with anyone else who may be in the reception area picking their patient up or just sit quietly until the door opens and she appears. The look for most of the time is smiling, but occasionally, now more often, she is upset or mad about something or someone who has "done her wrong." I do tend to think that sometimes some of those folks do get out of line.

Case in point: a gentleman at daycare, also with Alzheimer's, was following Helene around the facility, mistaking her for his wife. I guess he wasn't happy about something she did because he hauled her off and hit her in the face, knocking her glasses off, and she cried. The staff called me about the incident, as they always did if something went haywire, but she was fine and probably forgot about it shortly thereafter.

Helene tried to explain the problem on our way home, but getting the words out was becoming much more difficult. So I pretended to know exactly what she was saying and either nodded or said something like, "I would be mad too" or "I would not associate with him or her tomorrow." When we got home, I would ask her if she wanted a "sampler" which was some Triscuit crackers with hummus or cheese or herring on them and add a couple of slices of pepperoni. Usually, we'd have that with a little glass of wine for her and a Tanqueray martini for me before dinner. Now I give Helene some iced tea with a splash of lemonade in it instead of wine. I was afraid the alcohol would not be a good mix with her meds.

The meds still seem to be helping, but that could change daily. This month we are to see the last theater venue (her health put an end to it) at the Raleigh Little Theater. As I mentioned, we love theater (we have been to over 270 productions, from Broadway to local theater in our thirty years together—we saved the Play Bills). I get season tickets each year, but certain venues are in a small theater (they have three theaters in one building), some are of partial bleacher seats or chairs on different levels and Helene is afraid to climb to them, so I arrange to sit us in front row seats in a chair. After I explained the situation, they were happy to accommodate. After the theater, which is Sundays at 5:00 p.m., we usually went to an early dinner at a local restaurant. The last three plays for February, May, and June I gave my tickets to my caregivers to enjoy.

February 2017 we visited Dr. Z once again on the sixteenth. His judgment was to change to Zyprexia, as Helene's stability had drifted remarkably. Helene's two daughters flew down from Connecticut for a visit on the first weekend of February, so we didn't have caregivers that weekend. Helene was happy to see them but said little. The girls noticed an ever-declining health and ability to communicate. We dined out, but restaurants afforded no relief to any enjoyment.

February 14th was, you guessed it, Valentine's Day. I as usual bought her roses and a nice "mushy" card. Helene loved flowers. Since restaurants had become taboo, we had dinner at home.

Since Helene's former dentist was too far away now due to her condition, on Feb 22nd, I got one closer to home for both of us. Dr. E (lady dentist) had a very nice staff of women and a practice with all the bells and whistles. They took some X-rays and cleaned her teeth. They were aware of her condition and did everything to accommodate. Helene was happy and got done what they needed to do. The next appointment was scheduled in March.

On February 27th we had a haircut appointment with a hairdresser in Cary we had used only a few times. She was a lot closer than the one in Raleigh we had gone to and came well recommended from one of our neighbors who had gone to her for twenty years. I usually took Helene to these appointments after I picked her up from daycare. The appointment was for 4:30 p.m. and we got there 15 minutes early. The hairdresser was supposedly finishing up someone in her chair. Since there was no one left in the place but us, I expected to wait only a few minutes.

Our appointment time passed and Helene was getting a little antsy and asked me when she was getting her haircut. I knew sitting too long was not a good thing for her as anxiety starts taking over and she wants to go. At that point, 4:45 p.m., I got up and walked toward the hairdresser signaling toward my watch. She said just a few more minutes. I walked toward Helene and started looking at some of the hair products sitting neatly on shelves, thinking maybe I could divert her attention away from her anxiety, giving the hairdresser a chance to "finish up." We sat back down, now 5:00 p.m., hoping maybe another minute or so.

The hairdresser and her customer kept talking. Finally, at 5:15 p.m., after waiting for 45 minutes past our appointment and Helene getting nervous, I got us up and walked out. We never went back nor got an apology or call from that woman. She knew full well Helene's condition and yet found her conversation was more important. I guess there is no accounting for ignorance or disrespect.

At the end of February one of the two caregivers resigned. She told me she was pregnant and she could not take care of Helene since there was a possibility that since Helene had a propensity to hit without warning and her pregnancy was "at risk," getting hit in the stomach was something she wanted to avoid. I understood and knew I had to replace her.

March 2017. Since our original hairdresser appointment went badly, I decided to try our daycare hairdresser who had been in the business for many years. Helene went to daycare as usual in the morning. Her appointment was for 1:00 p.m. that afternoon, so I told her I would get there for her appointment so I could make sure

Helene was okay with it and I wanted to orchestrate and see the result.

When I got there, there was someone before Helene, so we waited until she was done. It took only a few minutes. I struck up a conversation with the hairdresser and she told me she spends 12-hour days going to different daycare and nursing homes in the surrounding towns doing both men's and women's hair. I was impressed with not only her work with Helene, but the number of hours per day spent making others happy.

March 13th we went to Dr. Z's office—Helene gets more upset when she sees him compared to other doctors. I guess it's having to do with the mind and she knows hers is not what it should be, but he has a great tissue supply, so I don't need to prepack them. Since he is right up the street from daycare, I pick her up there around noon, take her to see him, then take her back to daycare for lunch and the rest of the day. I then returned at 4:00 p.m. to pick her up as usual.

Helene's stability is worsening. Getting her in and out of the car and walking, even on level surfaces and short distances, is an effort. Her left leg seems to lag in back of her right. She seems to need to stop and think about moving it, but more of a shuffle is apparent.

March 14th we visited our new dentist again for a cleaning. This would be the last dentist appointment Helene would ever go to. The office was well air-conditioned and Helene complained about being cold, so she got the royal treatment with a blanket to make her comfortable enough to get and finish the cleaning.

March 16th (this was a busy week for doctors) our appointment was with Dr. B, the neurologist at Duke. I mentioned Helene's walking problem. The doctor took Helene for a walk to judge her stability and talk to her to see her state of mind. I sat in the office until they returned. I asked if this would be an appropriate time to take Helene off the two Alzheimer's drugs Namenda and Aricept since the illness was so far advanced and wondered whether the drugs were helping at all. He suggested to keep her on them for a while longer but recommended taking her off all vitamins and nonessential meds. Little did we know that day that we were close to removing most all of the medications.

March 17th I interviewed and hired my new caregiver from recommendations of my current one coming Saturdays. She was bright and smiling and willing to work. She wanted full-time. I said I wanted commitment, trust and punctuality, and a dedication to Helene. She agreed, and I said I'd be in touch. Little did I know I would need her very soon.

Saturday, March 18th my caregiver was coming from 10:00 a.m.–4:00 p.m. and I had a caregiver luncheon in Durham to attend. Helene and I were attending a Saint Patrick's Day dinner at the clubhouse at 5:30 p.m. that night. I hadn't heard from our usual group of friends we sat with, but I assumed they would be there as usual.

When we got to the clubhouse, I noted one of our friends was sitting at a full table. The others were not there. I went and asked him and he said the rest of our group weren't coming—they had other plans. So much for assuming. I then had a quandary: do I stay and sit with people Helene may not know or go home? Helene was more comfortable with the friends we usually sat with, even though her conversational skills were nonexistent, but since we paid in advance for the meal, I figured we'd give it a try.

I spied a table with two couples at it that seemed to be in heavy conversation. We went over and asked if they had others joining them. They said no, so we sat down and I introduced Helene and myself. They did likewise and continued their conversation with each other. I tried making small talk but to no avail. They must have been "related."

When each table was asked to go to the buffet, I asked the woman closest to Helene if she would mind staying at the table while I got both of our meals. She looked a bit annoyed but said she would. I told Helene I would be right back and went to the buffet line. Through the rest of the meal and dessert, the two couples kept on talking as though we weren't at the table. Every once in a while one of them would glance at Helene then me. Helene got uneasy so I told her we'd go home. Maybe they knew something I didn't —that this was the last time Helene would go to any function at the clubhouse.

March 23rd Helene had an appointment with Dr. R at 9:30 a.m. for a medical review and general check of her condition. I told him that we had seen Dr. B the previous week and that Dr. B suggested stopping the nonessentials. He agreed and took them from his list as well. I also mentioned the walking problem to him and he noted it. I then took Helene to daycare for the rest of the day. Helene's walking problem continued to deteriorate. Daycare called twice in the month of March due to her falls there. Fortunately, no major injuries were incurred.

On Wednesday, March 29th, I went to pick her up as usual at 4:00 p.m. Upon arriving, I discussed Helene's instability with staff and her inability to move one leg after another when walking. It appeared to me we were playing "Russian Roulette" each day with chances of her breaking a bone or head trauma.

One of the staff got Helene and brought her to the reception area. She was shuffling her feet with the left leg lagging behind the right. The nurse offered to assist me in getting Helene to the car using a gait belt (a heavy-duty belt similar to a belt used in the moving business to lift large pieces of furniture). I agreed and we opened the reception door to the sidewalk outside.

We both got Helene to the sidewalk, but she stopped and couldn't move. The daycare director then offered to assist by getting the car doors opened as the nurse and I slowly talked Helene through each step forward, holding the gait belt around her waist. When we finally reached the car, the next step was getting Helene turned so she was able to sit in the front seat, then lifting and turning her legs to fit inside the car.

This step was harder than I thought and the daycare director reached in from the driver's side and stabilized Helene while I lifted her legs and centered her in the front seat. At this point, the three of us looked at each other, a bit weary and knowing a new plateau had been reached. My thoughts at that point were, What happens when I get Helene home? Will I be able to get her in the house?

The director must have been reading my mind when she said, "Since I am leaving here soon, would you want me to follow you home and help?" She lived only a few miles from me, so I thought about it and declined her offer, saying I thought I could manage, but thanks. Later, I called her on her cell and told her after due consideration about Helene's instability and further chances of falling, I am, effective immediately, withdrawing her from daycare and bringing in caregivers to my home full time. She agreed and wished me well.

CHAPTER SIX
The 'A' Team is formed

April 1, 2017, my Saturday caregiver and CNA, Irene, was here as usual. She was very experienced in handling patients like Helene. Irene's maturity, being my senior member of the team, fit in well with Helene's needs. She was kind and understanding yet firm and "take charge." She often coordinated the team's schedule to make sure the coverage I needed was in place and if someone on the team couldn't do their normal schedule, she would offer to switch things around to accommodate all concerned. She would sit with Helene and talk to her as if they'd been friends for years. Irene had a big family and would often visit them for get-togethers either locally or upstate NY/NJ area.

I contacted my new hire of March 17th on March 30th and asked her to start full-time on Saturday, April 2nd. She agreed and Kenya became my second CNA member of the team. Kenya, or "Z" as she is sometimes called, because her first name begins with a Z, was bright and cheery all of the time. She seemed to sparkle even in the mornings when, for many people, a joyous "Good Morning, Paul, or Helene" would be a "throw a pillow over your head" announcement, but to me, it meant "Thank God she is here!" Helene was a bit more startled when she opened her eyes due to declining health, but still, I think welcomed her. She was all the things I had asked for in my employment interview and then some.

I was referred to my third team member CNA Latoya through Kenya. I desperately needed a person to be with Helene overnight for at least two nights a week, so I could get some sleep. Up until now, I was the only one with Helene from 4:30 p.m. that day until 8:30 a.m. the next day when Kenya arrived. At that time, we slept in the same king bed, but I couldn't go to our guest room due to her waking up a couple of times at night to either want to talk (incoherently) to me or take her to the bathroom due to her incontinence. I probably got an average of 3 hours of sleep a night for the last two years.

Latoya and Kenya were friends for many years and worked together on a number of assignments. Latoya interviewed with me on April 10th. She was much more reserved than Kenya in personality but had all of the fine qualities of the other two. She would arrive at 10:00 p.m. and stay until 7:00 a.m. the next morning. When I got up at 6:30 a.m., she had gotten Helene changed and ready for

Kenya to arrive at 8:30 a.m. These three amazing women helped me to make Helene's last days the best anyone could hope for.

The first two weeks of April 2017 were hectic since Helene was out of daycare and not walking very well. My 'A' team was still allowing me to attend to daily errands as well as my Duke Support Group meetings and luncheons. The walker I purchased last October was little used. Kenya would try to get Helene out for a short walk up and down the street, but she would have trouble getting stuck in the sidewalk cracks, get confused with operating the hand brakes, or decide she didn't want to go further after a half a block from the house.

My neighbor across the street saw what was going on from her window and asked if we'd like to borrow a wheelchair of hers, used a few years back for a leg injury, she had in her garage. She told me to use it as long as I needed it or until she did. I thanked her and brought it home, cleaned it up a bit, and started using it.

Both Kenya and I would take Helene out in the wheelchair, but even that did not seem to please her. On one occasion, one of our close friends who hadn't seen Helene in a while saw Kenya walking past her house with Helene in the wheelchair as she was driving around the corner. She stopped, got out of her car, came over to Kenya, and looked down at Helene, slumped in the chair. My neighbor started crying and told Kenya she almost didn't even recognize Helene in the state of health she was in. I considered buying (and did) a wheelchair ramp to get the chair out the door easier, but before I had a chance to use it I returned it, as we realized she couldn't use the chair anymore.

Due to her lack of walking ability, Helene was relegated more and more to the bed. Feeding her, cleaning her up, and going to the bathroom were much more difficult, especially from the king-sized platform bed we slept in. I then purchased a port-a-potty for her bedside. Turning her over to change her, many times, involved one of us standing at the bedside while the other had to climb onto the bed in a position to reach her, to say nothing of the changing of the protective bed-wetting pads necessary for the overnight hours.

Showers too were a nightmare. Since Helene couldn't navigate the shower anymore and got rather feisty in opposition to it, I purchased a shower chair. This chair was two-thirds in the tub and one-third outside it. The two of us had to sit her on the outside part of the shower chair, then coax her to lift her legs up and swing them into the tub part while positioning her body along the chair so the spray wouldn't get on the floor. Meanwhile, Helene's anxiety would get revved up and she would yell and pound the walls as if she were being beaten to death.

Eating was also difficult. Since solid foods weren't tolerable anymore, we would prepare cereals, yogurt, puddings, and Ensure chocolate drinks which had a lot of extra vitamins and minerals. She still was taking some of her prescriptions morning, noon, and nights.

During the second week of April, Kenya and I agreed that Helene needed to be looked at by hospice (Transitions Life Care). Kenya's experiences with other patients and Helene's general health deterioration spoke to our need to go to the next step. I put a call into our neurologist, Dr. B at Duke. One of his staff people, whom I knew from Duke Support, called me back and said she was filling out the paperwork and the doctor was sending a referral to hospice to come out and evaluate Helene's condition.

On April 16th we were visited by Transitions Hospice. An evaluation was done and on April 19th we received a letter from them verifying Helene's eligibility under Medicare for treatment.

CHAPTER SEVEN

The Final Days

On April 22, 2017, Helene entered into the complete care of Transitions Hospice Care through her Medicare eligibility. All services would be covered 100 percent and managed by Advanced Home Care, Inc. Any outside treatment, doctors, hospitals, medications, etc. must have the prior approval/card of Hospice and all billings would go directly to them. A full electric medical bed, bed rails, therapeutic mattress, and table overbed were delivered and set up.

All necessary supplies (including medications) would be delivered to our home as needed within 24 hours, via phone call to them. From April 22nd through month end, Kenya and I were ultimately introduced to the Transitions Team, which consisted of a manager, triage nurse, social worker, and spiritual counselor. Others would be available and in fact, did respond, when my assigned team was not. Helene received a case ID number which was used when calling in for supplies or services, and a DNR (Do Not Resuscitate Order) was placed above her bed.

Each team member visited, after the initial introduction (between April 24 and 26), either by my request or a set day Hospice chose to check up on us. All members of our Hospice team that came were very professional in their respective positions and offered their support whenever and wherever they could. This was a major relief to me and my "A" team.

Since the equipment delivery people were not allowed to assist in getting patients into their new bed, Kenya and I knew there would be a struggle to transport Helene from our king-sized bed in the master bedroom to the room I decided on, which was bright and facing the street near the front door. This would be the best for all of us and the Hospice Team agreed.

April 23rd, since Helene was no longer able to walk and moving her

met with a lot of anxiety, we decided to use the wheelchair as the vehicle to get her there instead of trying to carry her. Even with that, it would be a little tedious. We prepared the new bed with sheets, a blanket and mattress protector, then lowered the bed to transfer Helene more easily. We took a deep breath and headed toward the master bedroom.

As expected, trying to get Helene out of the king-sized bed was a struggle. I positioned the wheelchair while Kenya tried putting her in a sitting position. Then quickly Kenya faced her, grabbed Helene under her arms and turned her slightly while I got the chair under her butt and we sat her down. Wow! step one done.

Step two was to move Helene down the hall towards her new quarters in the wheelchair with some haste. We would move the wheelchair close to the bed, got on each side of her, stood her up enough to pick her up under her legs (fireman's carry), and placed her in bed. Sounds easy? No—all the time she was yelling at us and upset. Even in the same house, new surroundings were a bit unsettling. This room, unfortunately, would be Helene's home for the last twenty-eight days of her life.

For the remainder of April, Helene adjusted to her new quarters fairly quickly. The electric bed was the best present to me and my "A" team for feeding, sleeping, changing her and the bed, and washing her. We were able to raise and lower Helene with the push of a button.

We received the supplies we needed quickly such as diapers, chucks (protective disposable bed pads), personal wipes, mouth swabs, (used for tooth brushing), suppositories, milk of magnesia, and refrigerated drugs such as morphine. We set up the room to accommodate her supplies and a radio for music which was played daily on a station playing the oldies. The overbed table also came in handy to feed her, wash her, and even hold my meals as well. Kenya would get her meal together at night before she left at 4:30 p.m. Then I would make myself something, feed her, then myself. Sometimes we'd watch the news or a game show together on my iPad I put on the table.

May 2017 brought more decline in health. Helene's meals basically consisted of soft but nourishing foods such as oatmeal, yogurt, pudding, Ensure, juices, and ice cream. I usually did the dinner feedings while my "A" team did breakfast and lunch. I helped during the day if Kenya or Irene needed me to help change her or roll her, as bed sores are prevalent and constant changes in position as well as Desitin cream are necessary to alleviate them. Luckily, she never got them.

The Hospice team would come in and check Helene every couple of days. Our main concern was constipation due to the lack of solid foods and lying in the bed all the time. Hospice recommended she have bowel movement at least every three days. At first, even with stimulants like milk of magnesia or suppositories, no results were evident. At least three times, manual extraction was necessary to evacuate. Finally, with the combination of stimulants, we did get results. Otherwise, an enema was the answer.

Each day Helene got a little weaker. She was napping more during the day and at night, it was lights out at 7:30 p.m. Helene's breathing while sleeping was louder and very raspy due somewhat to her mouth being open while sleeping. Being constantly exhausted, I actually welcomed the early lights out for her so I could lie down, usually an hour later. The nights Latoya did not come, I slept in our guest bedroom which was closer to the room Helene was in.

Despite the early turn in for me, I didn't sleep much, listening for Helene to make a noise other than the normal or sometimes talking in her sleep. I was up two to three times per night checking on her. I was up at 6:30 a.m., got a shower, and then changed Helene. I called her "the wife of my life" or "my young bride" all the time. I would kiss her on the forehead, then gently on the lips and whisper, "I love you." She'd look up at me, usually smile, and say it back.

I grabbed some breakfast in the kitchen, then sat with Helene until Kenya or Irene would come. My "A" team and I spent many hours in that room. We'd listen to the oldies on the radio and talk about anything and everything. They became extended family. Helene didn't say much. She'd smile or say a yes or no when asked a question. Her waking hours mostly consisted of eating little and sleeping on and off.

Helene's daughters were supposed to visit us the last weekend of May to celebrate our wedding anniversary on the twenty-eighth. May was a very special month for Helene and me—we had Mother's Day, Helene's birthday on May 18th, and our anniversary. We usually did a big trip around the May/June time frame to celebrate. Our last trip was May 5th to the 15th, of 2014 to celebrate our twenty-fifth wedding anniversary. We went to Turkey and Israel (with side trips to Bethlehem and Jerusalem), then cruised the Mediterranean to Cyprus and Greece. We had traveled to so many places over the years, sometimes with family or friends. Each trip we planned together as we did with everything.

Hospice came a couple of times the weeks of May 8th and May 15th to check Helene's breathing and chest sounds. I could see they looked more worried the first week and said the chest sounds were not encouraging. I thought that I'd better call Laurie and Jennifer and tell them to forget about the last weekend of the month and get here ASAP the previous week instead. The signs were not good. They got back to me and said they were able to change the reservations to arrive on May 18th (Helene's birthday).

May 18th I picked the girls up at the airport around noon and drove home where Kenya was waiting. We filled the girls in on Hospice's conclusions that it wouldn't be too much longer. Helene at this point was breathing with mouth open, basically unresponsive.

May 19th the hospice nurse manager arrived in the morning, listened to Helene's breathing, and said they were going to start administering Ativan for anxiety and the Morphine to Helene by placing the liquid between her cheek and gum on the right side, to keep her relaxed and comfortable. She showed Kenya and me how it was done. The applications were to be administered one tablet every 4 hours for the Ativan and .5 mg every 3 hours for the Morphine until 1:00 p.m. then every hour on the hour thereafter. That evening after Kenya left, we set up a dosage chart and the girls said they would take over all through the night so I could get a little rest. I agreed and went to bed.

May 20th I woke up at about 6:00 a.m. and went to see how Helene was doing. The girls had taken turns all night giving Helene the meds. They looked beat. The three of us sat around the bed holding her hands, rubbing her arms or resting our heads on the bed near her. I kept checking Helene's curated artery for her pulse. Her breathing was slower now, mouth still open, and that raspy sound filled the room.

I looked at the 100-year-old pendulum clock on the wall that was given to Helene years ago by her family. It was 6:57 a.m. We looked at each other tired and sad. I again felt Helene's neck. She hesitated for a few seconds, took another breath, and then all was quiet. I felt her neck again — no pulse. I looked at the girls and said, "I think Mom is gone." It was 7:00 a.m.

We all started crying and holding Helene's hands. I kissed her forehead and said I was going to call for the hospice nurse. The nurse was coming from Durham so it took a while. The nurse arrived about 7:45 a.m., filled out a few papers, and took a few minutes to make sure Helene was gone. The nurse pronounced Helene's passing at 8:05 a.m.

Laurie and Jennifer, very upset, moved to another room. I stayed in the room with the nurse who had to call the funeral home to have Helene removed from the house. I sat in the room staring into space. The nurse was making calls and filling out more papers. At least a half hour to forty-five minutes went by, still waiting for the transport. The nurse made another call checking on the whereabouts of the transport. A few minutes later they arrived in an unmarked dark grey minivan.

Two men got out dressed in ties and jackets with the stretcher between them. I greeted them at the front door and pointed to the room Helene was lying in. I stayed in the foyer near the front door watching them as they prepared to put her on the stretcher. They said little but I could tell they had done this many times before. First a white silky sheet was wrapped over her, then she was placed on the stretcher. Next they covered her with a dark blue velvet or velour blanket.

I backed away from their path and went to check on the girls. They were in another room grieving. I returned to the room Helene was in and they were gone, but in her place on the bed was that one centered pink faux rose. The nurse then quietly exited from the house. I drove the girls to the airport later that day.

On May 22nd, the home care company came to retrieve the four items they had delivered a month earlier. The "wife of my life" was gone.

On May 27th my oldest daughter Kim arrived from Florida to visit and stayed until Memorial Day the 29th. I think she may have been worried about me. I was glad to see her. She was a lot like me—always joking, hardworking, a lot of fun to be with, and a real-people person. We talked and ate out. We went to a movie venue (CineBistro) where you order a dinner off a menu and eat it while the movie is going on (she treated). I drove her to Helene's grave site and showed her the columbarium where Helene would be interned in June. She said she would be back to help on June 10th.

CHAPTER EIGHT
The Celebration of a Life

Helene and I both believed each life should be celebrated with those they have known and loved upon leaving this earth. In that spirit, both of us wrote down our wishes in planning our final exit, besides the normal wills and funeral arrangements. Essentially we wanted the same thing: to be remembered at a gathering of those who knew us and those who loved us at our community clubhouse.

The week after Helene's death, I called my friends in the Social Committee about arranging for the celebration for Helene at the clubhouse. We knew many people in this community after seven years here and felt a closeness that we wanted to share. We had been to other celebrations in the clubhouse over the years and knew the committees did an excellent job.

Basically, my responsibilities were to estimate the number of people coming for both table and seating accommodations, food ordering, and the logistics of program timing, pictures, memorial video, and sign-in register. The desserts, beverages including soft drinks and coffee, table set up, microphones, speaker's dais, and projectors were all handled by our Social Committee.

After talking to our on-site property manager about when the room would be available, we settled on Sunday, June 11th from 2:00–4:00 p.m., which gave me two weeks to contact our friends both in and out of state, the funeral home, caterer, and Cremation Society. Since Helene and I had already prepaid for our funeral arrangements when we moved to North Carolina, it was just a matter of coordinating the timing of events for cemetery internment, obituary notices in newspapers (both in CT and NC), memorial cards, and pictures for the memorial video. I coordinated with Helene's daughter Laurie in CT to work with the Creation Society for the memorial cards, video, and obituary notice. On June 5th I ordered the food (sandwiches, fruits, etc. for 100 guests).

June 8th my close friends Stan and Kathy from Connecticut arrived. They stayed at a motel in the town next to mine. We had spent many years as friends. Kathy also worked in the same hospital that Helene did. We were able to spend a little time together.

June 10th both Kim and Laurie arrived. They stayed with me at the house. I had arranged for an internment at 2:30 p.m. that afternoon at the cemetery. I had called a couple of days in advance so they would open the niche and be prepared to accommodate seating for a small gathering of my closest friends and relatives.

Afterwards, they would join me at a nearby restaurant— I had made reservations for and have lunch. There were eleven of us, including the neighbors on either side of me and the first couple we befriended in the community. My other two close friends from Florida, Harold, and Sandy, called and said they would be arriving late but would meet us at the restaurant when they arrived.

The cemetery was only a couple of miles from the house. When we moved to North Carolina it was still under construction. The niche was an octagon-shaped marble with praying hands at the top, sitting on a circle of brick close to the main entrance. The cemetery was nicely done and had a rather large mausoleum.

When we arrived, the owner was waiting for us. He had already removed the marble that revealed the space Helene's ashes would be placed in and eventually, my own. The space was about shoulder height so no bending was involved. Our plaques were already mounted on the marble for both of us, all that was remaining to be filled from mine was the end date. There was enough seating for everyone. They even had marble seats surrounding the niche as well.

There were no clergy present, but I did plan on reading two short poems I found online appropriate for the occasion. The first one was called, "When God Saw You Getting Tired." It went like this:

> When God saw you getting tired
> And a cure was not to be
> He put his arms around you
> And whispered come to me
> He didn't like what you went through
> And he gave you rest
> His garden must be beautiful
> He only takes the best
> And when we saw you sleeping
> So peaceful and free from pain
> We wouldn't wish you back
> To suffer that again
> Today we say goodbye
> And as you take your final rest
> That garden must be beautiful
> Because you are one of the best.

The second poem I read was called, "Do not Stand at My Grave and Weep" and it went like this:

> Do not stand at my grave and weep
> I am not there.
> I do not sleep.

I am a thousand winds that blow
I am the diamond glints on snow,
I am the sunlight on ripened grain,
I am the gentle autumn rain.
When you awaken in the morning's hush,
I am the swift uplifting rush,
Of quiet birds in circled flight,
I am the soft stars that shine at night,
Do not stand at my grave and cry,
I am not there; I did not die.

I got through the two poems with some hesitation, as my sadness came through and my throat had that large lump in it. When I finished, I asked if anyone wanted to say anything. My audience was quiet. I then signaled to Laurie to stand next to me and her mother's ashes sitting on a small table in a rectangular brass metal box. Together we touched the box, and everyone bowed their heads and said their own silent prayer.

Everyone then headed to their cars. I stayed behind for a few minutes. The owner of the cemetery then placed the box in the niche and stepped back. I reached my hand out to touch it once more. I bowed my head and said the 23 Psalm in silence. I then followed everyone to the cars and headed to the restaurant.

Chapter Eight

The gathering at the restaurant was a bit quiet. My friends from Florida did get there, so all the friends and family I was closest to joined me in a toast to Helene.

June 11th, the big day. The celebration in the clubhouse was to start at 2:00 p.m. I woke up early at about 6:30 a.m. and felt a little nervous that everything would be done the way I had planned. I had plenty of support I know, but nonetheless, I wanted our tribute to Helene to be perfect. Kim and Laurie got up about 8:30 a.m. and I suggested we have breakfast out. A breakfast/lunch-only restaurant opened up nearby recently and it was good.

At breakfast, we talked about the setup at the clubhouse and thought about putting a random variety of photos on a tack board and labeling them for year and occasion. This would be placed on an easel stand at the entrance to the meeting room we would be in since many people there would not know those with Helene. When we got home I grabbed a few boxes of photos and the three of us went through them and picked out about twenty-five to thirty different years, places, and people in the pictures with Helene. We made labels and stuck them on the bottoms of the photos.

Around 11:30 a.m. I was getting a little fidgety and asked Kim and Laurie to come to the clubhouse with me and start setting things up. It was a bit early, but I needed to keep busy. We drove over, got the things out of the car, and walked in.

I was surprised to find the ladies of the social committee this early there busily getting the tables arranged, the kitchen set up for the food, to say nothing of the many homemade desserts, the tablecloths on, with flowers in vases on each table. Even Kim got in the mix and helped the ladies with the tablecloths. One of the many reasons Helene and I loved this community was the friendships and helping hands in times of need. We set to work getting the tack board set up. The girls started on that, while I attended to the memorial video and microphone setup with one of the ladies who knew how to run it. We even played the video to make sure it would loop properly. I then got out the podium for speakers and stood to hold our guest registry to sign as people came in. We placed one of Helene's framed pictures, memorial cards, a speakers signup sheet, a copy of Helene's obituary, and the memorial photo book Laurie had done on the table in the foyer.

A large, beautiful bouquet of all-white flowers mounted on a stand was delivered from my Citizens Volunteer Police Organization and placed inside next to the front door of the clubhouse. The food was delivered just before 1:00 p.m. as requested. I looked around—everything seemed to be ready. I just hoped I was.

Just before 2:00 p.m., people started arriving. I stood at the entrance of the big room greeting everyone I could. After the first ten minutes or so, I found myself drifting throughout the foyer shaking hands and hugging. As friends started toward me I tried to engage them, leaving the arms of one to be hugged again by another.

I kept asking each to sign my guest book, hoping they would accommodate, so later on I could read each name and know they cared. Laurie and Kim were also floating around the room introducing themselves, shaking hands, and hugging.

A couple of the committee ladies approached and asked me about food and seating announcements to get the celebration underway since we had only two hours and people were still coming in. I told them to make the announcements for both. I gave it another ten minutes or so, then took the microphone and stood at the podium, took a deep breath, and started my welcome.

I looked around the room—it was packed. I was grateful that so many came for Helene. I was so proud to be her husband. I introduced the two tables that sat my family and closest friends. Some came from Massachusetts, Connecticut, Florida, and Pennsylvania. All loved her enough to be here.

Then came my Duke Support Group, Transitions Life Care, my "A" team, my daycare, my Citizens Volunteer Police Group, and last but not least, my community's Social Committee who helped me put this celebration on. All these people contributed to supporting me in the care of someone I cherished.

I then read the two written memories by the daughters Helene loved so dearly. The first was from her youngest, Jennifer. She had written this prior to Helene's death and gave it to me the weekend Helene died. I read it and told her it didn't need fixing—it was perfect. It's worth reading.

"It's strange to look back now and remember all of the incredible things about our mom. I feel almost resentful of my youth. Growing up I didn't understand how much she really did. I can't say that I cared to know. But now I stand here telling all of you how incredible she was and wish I had the sense to tell her such a long time ago.

"All of you who knew our mom knew her caring, loving, and kind nature, but what you may not know is that she was an activist long before activists were a thing.

"Growing up, I had no idea that having Fresh Air Fund Kids from inner cities stay with us each summer was strange. I didn't know that having foreign exchange students living with us was not normal. Our family photos include some wonderful ladies from Japan, a few from England, and a Russian gentleman named Boris. Mom not only welcomed all of these cultures into our home, she relished it. She believed in equality even when it was unpopular, and she led by example.

"It took great strength and courage at times to have an open home the way she did—not everyone was so accepting. But it didn't stop there. She was in the League of Women Voters, the Monroe Jaycees, and later the Friends of the Monroe Library. Even later she and Dad volunteered at the Monroe Library during tax season.

"Mom was reserved, but just because she spoke quietly didn't diminish her. She felt strongly and passionately about equality, about women's rights, and the right to a good education for everyone. It was these convictions that gave her the inner strength she needed to raise two spirited teenage daughters in a town and at a time that frowned upon families of divorce and often judged women harshly for their perceived failings.

"Just getting a credit card for a woman after a divorce was a job in and of itself back then. Women, while they could vote, get an education, and enter the workforce—it seemed they could not handle their own finances. They could not be successful breadwinners and caretakers of their families. There were many naysayers our mother had to fight and that stigma took years, decades, to be snuffed out, but she never gave up and never caved in.

"She started college at eighteen years old, but left to work full time and raise a family. But her desire for education never waned and she returned to college as a part-time student and earned her college degree in 1985. She worked full time, went to college, raised two kids, volunteered with her many organizations, all the while hoping to meet someone she could love and spend her life with. It was long into my adult years when I began to fully realize the strength she'd possessed and the sacrifices she made.

"I'd like to tell her how proud I was of her, how she inspired me, how I know that she used to let me win the races to the car we had when running errands. But these thoughts only became pressing when we realized we were losing the chance to tell her.

"I think of her smile, the monkey face she would make, her long-running joke about her 'third child' —named 'I don't know' who was always the mischievous one. She could be very silly, and I loved her for that. We were the three Musketeers. Along with the pets she indulged us in. She always had many friends and I considered myself as one of them.

"One thing that may surprise everyone is that she was a great believer in alchemy—magic that can turn an object into another object! I know this because every single time I asked her to make me something, "Mom, make me an English muffin," she'd always say, "Poof, you're an English Muffin!" No matter what I asked, it was poof..

"I thank God that Mom found her soulmate in our dad, in Paul, her greatest achievement. Together they lived more in any given year than many couples do in a lifetime. They traveled, they volunteered, they entertained, but most importantly they loved. Their love was a light, a guide to what things could be. A life of love and harmony.

"In the end, that love never faltered, never waned even in the darkest moments, even in the end when Dad had to carry that love for the two of them. Today we are left with this bond, our dad Paul, me and my sister. The three who loved her the most. The three who will always remember how very special my mother was."

Laurie's memorial was remembering more good times later as an adult. She wrote the following: "The bond between a mother and child is often referred to as universal, but they are unique as well. My mother was my friend before she was my parent. She knew my secrets. She accepted me even when she disagreed, smiling at me while rolling her eyes.

"I got many things from my mother—a love of traveling, show tunes, silly jokes, Barry Manilow, reading, going to plays, and the color beige. I'd love to think I gave her things as well, but I believe my biggest accomplishment was getting her to admit to liking a David Bowie song."

"Our travels were significant. Besides trips within the States, I've been to five other countries with my mother. Sometimes planned and other times on a whim we would invite ourselves into one another's vacations. I think the funniest was our trip to California.

"Our intent was to drive up to San Francisco from San Jose. Well, I drove she navigated, neither of us knowing right from left, which somehow led to us driving right past San Francisco, over the Golden Gate Bridge—back when I had a fear of bridges. We ended up going over that blasted bridge four times and just laughing. I remember standing on the corner of Haight & Ashbury, wondering why this was still significant. I dragged her into every jewelry shop, she dragged me into any art show in Sausalito. We snacked at Ghirardelli's and rode the trolley car. At nights she let me keep the hotel window open so I could listen to the sea lions bark. Each morning she'd try to marry me off to the doorman. At the end of the trip, we wound up picking out the very same brown sweatshirt as personal souvenirs. She graciously let me keep my choice and she settled for a heather green version. After twenty-five-plus years we both still wore our shirts.

"I credit my mother with my best traits. She knew me in a way others don't or ever will. For the last few years, I called her every night to tell her I loved her. I miss those calls. My days are incomplete without her."

There were times reading each memorial I had to pause and wait for that apple stuck in my throat to leave, but I got through it. We had two speakers on my list. The first was my friend from Connecticut, Stan, who talked about the four of us and the good times we had over the years. From dinners to plays, to vacations, to cookouts, to New Year Eves, we stayed together. The other speaker was Helene's nephew Andrew. He, like his two brothers, father, and mother were very smart people. Andrew went to law school at UNC and passed the bar exam the first time. He spoke about our get-togethers for dinners at our house or restaurants and his admiration for the both of us being there for him since his family lived in Pennsylvania.

I closed the celebration by thanking Laurie for the memorial video and everyone for coming. Many came up to me and said how wonderful the celebration was. I just hope Helene liked it too.

The daughters flew home to CT or FL that evening. My friends and other family members started back that day or the following one. They all drove. I was mentally and physically exhausted, but relieved knowing I did my best.

My life with my wife Helene was a journey well worth taking. Almost from the moment I met her, some thirty-two years ago, I think we both knew it was right. Being in a relationship that grew stronger each day through a constant awareness of each other's needs, hopes, and dreams made everything possible. We laughed a lot, dreamed a lot, and disagreed little. We held hands a lot, hugged a lot, smiled at each other often, and kissed spontaneously. It was that good! Someone once said, "Life is not measured by the number of breaths we take, but by the moments that take your breath away."

Taking care of her as she disappeared from me for the last six years was the hardest thing I will ever do. When anybody ever asked me what our secret to success was in the marriage, I would always tell them there are three things you must do to make it great; share, respect, and communicate—it will all equal Love.

You may wonder what comes next for a caregiver after an ordeal like this. I guess it all depends on the caregiver. For me at least, I want to get back in the game of life. It may take a while longer, but traveling, volunteering, and maybe even finding someone to share life with again is not out of the question for me. When you have loved well as I have, being alone would not be my choice.

www.ingramcontent.com/pod-product-compliance
Lightning Source LLC
Chambersburg PA
CBHW060849050426
42453CB00008B/905